This book belongs to·

In memory of my beloved son Joshua.

He was just 2 1/2 years old the afternoon he slipped out of our sight those few moments. Minutes later, when we found him in the backyard pool, he was unconscious. He passed away 3 days later due to complications from drowning. I thought I had taken every precaution, installing a fence, pool cover, even a security camera. We tell our children to look both ways for cars, don't touch that stove, it's hot, and hold on to the handrail. We always think we will be with them when they are around water, but believe me, there are times when we may not be. Start early, add it to your list of educational warnings for your children. Water can be fun but **ONLY** when we are all **TOGETHER!** I hope many children can enjoy and learn from this story about a baby otter named Josh, and how he learns to be safe while in the water. Please read it again and again, and every time you finish give them a big hug and kiss.

Josh The Baby Otter

A tale promoting water safety for children

Written by Blake Collingsworth   Illustrated by Ashley Spitsnogle

It is a bright sunny morning.
The water is sparkling and a raft of
otters are very excited.

There is a new baby otter!

Josh

Alex, the otter, swims over to the new
baby's mother and says,
"He's a cute little guy.
What is his name?"

"His name is Josh," says Clare.
"I like that name. Can he come play with my buddy Austin and me?" asks Alex.
"It will be a while, because he must first learn to float. This will help him become a really good swimmer.
Then he will be able to play with you and Austin."

"Everyone should learn to float,"
says Josh's mother.
"Why?" asks Alex.
"When we get too tired, or the
waters are too rough to swim, we
can roll on our backs, look up at
the sky, relax and float."

"One of the very first things otters teach their babies, is how to float. This keeps them safe in the water."

"I don't remember learning to float,"
says Alex.
"That is because you were taught at a
very young age," says Clare.

"Was it hard for me to learn?"
asks Alex.
"Actually, you learned quite
quickly and until you learned you
were always with an adult.
You practiced a lot while being
held and supported," says Clare.

"Soon you were floating on your own, but someone was always by your side. You should **NEVER EVER** float or swim by yourself."

"Even when you're a good swimmer, **make sure** an adult is close by, and you should **ALWAYS** swim with a buddy!"

"Austin and I always swim together," answered Alex.
"Can we be Josh's swimming buddies?"
"That would be very nice, thank you for asking." replies Clare.

Alex hears his mother Nicole
calling...

"Alex come here. It's time
for dinner."

"Can I bring Austin by later to see
Josh?" asks Alex.
"Sure," says Josh's mother.
"You are always
welcome here."

Alex swims off.
"See you later," he says.

"See you later," says Clare.

Here comes Alex and Austin...

"Hi, Clare," says Alex.

"Hello, boys," says Clare.
"You are right, Alex, he IS a cute
little guy," says Austin.
"Can he play with us?" asks Austin.

"Oh no, not yet," answers Clare.
"Josh is finishing his floating
lessons. Would you boys like to
help me with Josh?"

"That would be great!" says Alex.

"I'm getting ready to let Josh float on his own. Can the two of you float by his side and hold his paws?" asks Josh's mother.
"Sure," says Alex.

Austin seems a little scared.
"It's okay, Austin, **I will be right here with the three of you the whole time**," assures Clare.

Clare slowly floats away from Josh while
Alex and Austin hold his paws,
so he won't float away.
"Yeah!" says Alex.
"He's floating by himself!" yells Austin.

"Now that he is floating he can start learning to swim," says Clare. Would you boys like to help me with his swimming lessons too?"

"Oh yes!" they say excitedly.

"We can begin tomorrow.
Be here bright and early in the morning,
and we will get started."

Alex and Austin are very excited and swim off to tell their parents.

"See you in the morning." says Austin.

"Thanks Clare." says Alex.

"You're welcome boys, see you tomorrow!"

Even though they do not remember learning, Alex and Austin have been reminded how important it is to try new things. Floating is the first thing you should learn if you want to be in the water. With a few lessons and a little time, you too can learn to float like Josh. Remember to always stay away from water unless you are with an adult. We all want you to be safe just like Josh.

*A note to all parents, grandparents, aunts, uncles,
and anyone in the care of young children.
The Joshua Collingsworth Memorial
Foundation asks you to please learn about
infant and toddler water training classes.
There are many fine organizations
and businesses throughout the country that offer this
specialized training. If your child can crawl,
they can learn to float on their back. The training
is not a long process and is usually
inexpensive. This training is also the first step in
your child's future enjoyment of learning to swim.
Most importantly, these classes could save their life.
Children can slip out of your sight for only a few
minutes, and in these precious moments,
if they are able to float, that could
give someone the opportunity to save them.
Please visit Joshua's website to learn
more about these classes. www.joshuamemorial.org*

Learn to Float

Josh the Otter water safety pledge

I promise to be a good son or daughter,

I promise to get an adult when I go near the water,

This will keep me safe like Josh the baby otter.

What You Otter Know About Otters

FuN oTTeR fAcTs

- Baby otters are called 'Pups' and are born in a den and not in the water.
- Otters teach their young how to swim like humans!
- There are 13 Different otter species around the world!
- Otters live on every continent except Australia and Antarctica.
- Otters live on both land and water.
- They have been around for nearly 5 million years!
- Otters are social and enjoy playing with each other just like us.
- They are one of the few animals that use tools.

SpEcIeS

Giant Otter
North American River Otter
Marine Otter
Southern River Otter
Neotropical River Otter
Sea Otter
Spotted-Necked Otter
European Otter
Hairy-Nosed Otter
Japanese Otter
African Clawless Otter
Oriental Small-Clawed Otter
Smooth-Coated Otter

Doing what you Otter with Water Safety Tips...

____ **Don't rely** on flotation devices as a substitution for supervision.

____ Assign a **water watcher** to monitor children during social gatherings

____ Keep **toys away** from pool area that might attract children

____ **Always** have **life saving equipment** readily available around pools

____ Post **CPR instructions** and assure adults and child care givers **know how to administrate** it

____ Make sure all **gates** are **closed and locked** when pool is not in use

____ Keep pool **covered** when not in use

____ **Teach** your children water safety and to always **stay away** from water unless they are **with an adult**

____ Stress that the last person to leave the pool area **closes** the gates, doors, and covers the pool before leaving the area

____ **Never leave children unattended**, even for a moment, around water

____ Keep a **phone** near the pool when in use. Call 911 in case of an emergency

Partners in Prevention

Families United To Prevent Drowning

Abbey's Hope Charitable Foundation
Because of B.R.A.Y.D.E.N.
Blake Sutor Water Safety Foundation
Blake's Miracle
CEF Foundation
Colin's Hope
Connor Cares Foundation
Elizabeth Bottorf Memorial Foundation
Fajr Memorial Foundation
Hannah's Foundation
Hope4JD
Jack Helbig Memorial Foundation
Just Against Children's Drowning

The BMF Project
The C.L.A.Y. Foundation
The Josh Project
The Katelyn Foundation
Trevor "Birdie" Davis Water Safety Foundation
Zac Foundation
LV Project
Mason's Gift
Mackenzie's Mission, Inc.
McGovern Foundation
Samuel Morris Foundation
Shallow Water Blackout Prevention
Stew Leonard III Children's Charities

www.joshuamemorial.org